The only thing that makes sense
is to grow

The only thing that makes sense is to grow

poems by
Scott Ferry

- 2020 -

The only thing that makes sense is to grow
© Copyright 2020 Scott Ferry
All rights reserved. No part of this book may be used or reproduced in any manner whatsoever without written permission from either the author or the publisher, except in the case of credited epigraphs or brief quotations embedded in articles or reviews.

Editor-in-chief
Eric Morago

Associate Editors
José Enrique Medina & Natalie Del Toro

Editor Emeritus
Michael Miller

Marketing Director
Dania Alkhouli

Marketing Assistant
Ellen Webre

Proofreader
Jim Hoggatt

Front cover art
Scott Ferry

Author photo
Molly Ferry

Book design
Michael Wada

Moon Tide logo design
Abraham Gomez

The only thing that makes sense is to grow
is published by Moon Tide Press

Moon Tide Press #166
6745 Washington Ave., Whittier, CA 90601
www.moontidepress.com

FIRST EDITION
Printed in the United States of America
ISBN # 978-1-7339493-5-4

for Lyle Ferry

Contents

Foreword by Alexandra Umlas	8
The only thing that makes sense is to grow	13
The fuchsia wand	14
Another time, another wand	15
Back when I was lying	16
Chant	17
Just rest	18
At 48	19
Free loop	20
Leave me be	21
Another one, or snip	22
I don't know the name	23
Let's eat ice cream and fly a kite!	24
My mother calls me	25
If I had a ticket	26
The way my father ate chicken	27
Red on the head	28
Did I tell you the story	29
My mother always beat my father at chess	31
Eggs	32
Dågan	33
Sunset through the wires	34
After the asking and getting of the things	35
Weeds, suffering	36
Seven pale rocks	37
Choices	39
Dice, marigolds, molecules	40
Naegleria Fowleri	41
Keyring	42
Ligaments, death	43
I guess at the end	44
Conversation	45
Other things Aunt Vernie told us	46
Pencil drawing from a photograph: the Ploosters ca. 1908	47
Alice and the plate	48
When I was 22	49
Driving from UC Santa Barbara	51

Michelle and I sit in the meditation room	52
My sister bought me a psychic reading	53
Safety card	54
Breathing	55
It is April again	56
Early June	57
Acknowledgements	58
About the Author	59

Foreword

"In the universe, there are things that are known, and things that are unknown, and in between them, there are doors."

— William Blake

Liminal spaces occur when there is a threshold between two worlds, like the space between not existing and being born, or the space between being a child and becoming an adult, or the strange stretch of space between life and death. Reading poet Scott Ferry's first collection of poems, *The only thing that makes sense is to grow*, feels like sitting in the living room of the liminal. Ferry magically captures and roots to the page life's slippery in-betweens and how they manage to stay with us, comforting us, haunting us, and often doing both at once.

The collection opens with a title poem that captures the essence of thresholds. A father, who is "decaying," and a daughter who is springing with life, go into their garden to plant seeds. The garden here is an apt metaphor for transitions—the seeds go into grave-like planters like "new limbs into cold earth." Paradoxically, in the poem the aging father is childlike, while the young child is wise and certain in her planting. Ferry's title, "The only thing that makes sense is to grow," captures one thing we can cling to regardless of our circumstances—growth. Growing *is* what makes sense. We do it from the moment we are born, we do it from the lessons we learn after we are physically "grown," and, we even do it after death, becoming the material by which other things will eventually grow.

However, while Ferry's poems speak to growing and of those astonishing spaces in between changes, they also contain the vivid material of childhood memories, memories we never quite grow out of. Being a parent does have a way of making a person think about how he or she was parented, and poems about Ferry's daughter are interspersed with poems about his own father or of other family members, like a great aunt that, like Ferry, can "sense the dead." The poems themselves hold us in a sort of liminal space, where we are able to be both in the real world, and simultaneously in a poem-world built from language, surrounded by and introduced to the people and happenings that make up a life. Ferry gifts us with blunt yet beautiful recounting of his own life's experiences; and these experiences form connections, threading the dead to the living and the living to the not-yet-born. You very well may see your own childhood, your own child, or your own dead, in Ferry's poems. Perhaps life itself is the most liminal space of them all – a space in which we get to exist for a relatively brief amount of time. Ferry's poems tie us to this space, delivering to us the very thing Robert Frost states poetry can do in "The Figure a Poem Makes," which is to provide a "momentary stay against confusion."

Even as Ferry's words offer us these moments of clarity and of cohesion, they also contain their own liminality. We don't know how the next word will change the meaning of the one that comes before it. Because of this, poetry takes a certain bravery, a willingness to put something out into the world that will take on a life of its own. Writing, in this way, is very much like creating life. In the last poem of the collection, "Early June," Ferry describes the possibility of being a parent again, and when his wife asks him if he's scared, he replies, "I would not call it scared, / I would call it dread." The poems here capture both the brightness in life— the loving act of making perfect eggs, or the child who plays a song on her new ukulele; while also capturing the dread that lurks around each of life's bends— the dead that are still among us, the garden that refuses to flourish, the brain-eating amoeba that is skulking in our tap water.

Ferry's poems assert again and again poetry's ability to attach us firmly to life through language. His poems don't try to appease us. Instead, they are a reminder that we are all made of what has come before, and that we all too will eventually die—the cycle continuing, as it always has, new life springing up from what has been. We do find comfort in these poems, in the way that life overlaps with death, and in the way that growing becomes an imperative—something we must do because it is, after all, the only thing that makes sense. Your time will be well spent in the generous garden that is Ferry's collection, each poem rising out of the page's terrain like a magnificent tendril of hope.

— Alexandra Umlas
Huntington Beach, 2019

*To climb these coming crests
one word to you, to
you and your children:*

*"stay together
learn the flowers
go light"*

— Gary Snyder

The only thing that makes sense is to grow

My body struggles to make full sentences,
especially the first few steps out of bed
and down the hall with my daughter
clinging to my shoulders like a coil of questions.
She springs into the chair; I pretend to own my knees.
I cannot regenerate cartilage. I am decaying.

But I have built three long wooden boxes
that look like graves. I plan to place bags of dead
material enriched with peat moss and blood meal
and bovine manure into the caskets. She helps me
fill small black plastic trays with compost.
She monologues about flowers never being weeds,
as her fingers push seeds into each pod of dark soil.
I scribble on blue tape and attach to each group of cells:
marigold, leek, tomato, jalapeño, Cinderella pumpkin,
zucchini, broccoli, snow pea, sugar snap, sunflower,
echinacea, thimbleberry, apple, curly lettuce.
Some seeds are so small they are like mist,
some are as big as dried teeth.

We make her a spray bottle so she can drizzle
each container in her dew, singing bright drops
of youth that scatter with the droplets. Soon
peas jut out towards the skylights, followed by squashes
and sunflowers. She never wears a jacket outside,
even on this windy April afternoon, where we place
new limbs into cold earth. We hope
they will survive those unexpected lows.

The fuchsia wand

During Easter break I try to take my daughter
to the pool every day. Tuesday, she charges into
the water with a wand the color of all the sunsets
I don't get to watch with her, because I work
until after dark. She plows around the shallow end
like a frantic narwhal, a plastic star breaking any doubt.
She waves it at me with some authority and transforms me
into a *kitty with a mermaid tail.* I meow and dolphin kick.
Then she hops on my back and orders me: *swim underwater
as fast as when you were young.* Oh, really? That's doubtful.
Swim in the way I point the wand. So, I breaststroke and watch
for direction from above. We curve a slow C to the right,
then she breaks the arc and we go almost backwards
and complete another mirror C until we are back
under the lifeguard. *Do you know what we did?* She
asks with Hermione-eyes. *What?* I have to hear this.
We made a heart!
                        Yes. Yes we did. I don't know
how to respond, so I swing her around and put my whole
squeeze into her. My ear deforms in her face, I hug
her so resoundingly. She giggles and otters off
to the blue mat and I am thinking this could cure cancer
or melt clinical depression or stop people from killing.
And it was so easy. I try to hide that I am crying
from the adults by forcing on my goggles and
pretending to swim in a logical direction.

Another time, another wand

Yes, Leilani, I will die, hopefully, *hopefully*
before you. You will be in your late thirties or
if I'm lucky, maybe even in your fifties.

If I have taught you what I wish you to know,
you will believe that I am still here, even
though my body broke.

Thank God you still have your mother.
Jesus, Molly, you better still be radiating
the quiet light of a thousand pearls

like you do every day. (Oh Lord, this
is terrible to write. Why am I writing this?)
My daughter, I want you to remember

that Tuesday when we swam a heart,
when you Paso Dobled me with a sunset
star across the jaded floor of my mind.

I want you to know that I am cradling
your adult shoulders the same way,
now that my spirit is a child again.

Not in a creepy gargoyle or succubus way,
but the way my father approaches me
in the shower, full of lavender smoke

and after-snow clarity, and when I doubt
he reminds me that clocks and flesh do not
represent reality in the long hollow vessels

of the soul. I wish to hold you in these times
with the same tenderness. I hope you will
recognize the faint sweep of a wand

above you in the liquid of the sky.

Back when I was lying

to my wife about my addiction, almost three
years ago now, the fir-and-metal-rimmed skyline
held reverse potential, eyes rusted with scripts.

To appear to the person I loved
as something other than myself
was like touching her open skin
with somebody else's hands.

Every intention, even if good, apparated,
dissolved. The container cranes
and concrete beams of the viaduct
reminded me they could be gone
instantly tomorrow, so they stood
half-erased, flickering.

Then the worst thing happened
and there was no more deception,
just shame, and the roots and branches
connected and blackened.

They almost left, first my wife then my daughter
with her. Being left is worse than dying
because at least they would still
love me if I died.

Chant

As a child I used to be terrified of going to bed alone.
I would repeat *I don't want to see a ghost*
mouthing the words as if the departed could hear,
take pity on me, and decide not to materialize,

climbing reluctantly up the mirrored staircase
and back into the opal oven of light.
I don't know what made me think spirits
would take an interest in appearing

to an over-imaginative boy
gripping his Star Wars sheets
and chanting that same sentence to the dark.
I wonder if my grandfather ever crept low behind me,

breathing the breath of the dead on my neck,
blowing soft moths in my ears,
just to see what I would do,
his sly grin a hologram.

God knows I was already
prepared to see the skin of the room
tear open suddenly like a silver lung.
Thank you for not doing that,

grandfather. Just in case
you were about to. Still.

Just rest

11:38, then 12:21, the red of the alarm clock
keeps repeating my failures to sleep. Tomorrow,
I mean today, I swim in the Junior Olympics.
I am 12, and I should, by estimation
of my father, be in the finals of many

of my events. My intestines burl
with numbers and the phrases
which drain all the color when spoken:
you should have kicked off the wall,
you should reach,

you don't need to breathe near the finish.
All words my father speaks after I have
swum even a best time. The effort is never
enough, never perfected enough for a hug
or a compliment or a feeling of acceptance,

much less love. I go to my mother this night,
digital numerals escalating. She sees me at the side
of her bed, nudging her, a flat ghost. She lifts begrudgingly
into my room. *Even if you are not sleeping, you are resting.*
Just rest, it will be good enough. This proves inadequate

advice, she must know. She trudges back to bed.
The last number to burn my eyes is 3:18. We drive
past the mall that looks like Babylonia on our way to East LA.
The rounded oxen and curled beards make me want
to vomit. Maybe if we get in a car wreck, or our Impala fails

I won't have to compete. Maybe I won't have to hear
about all the things I always should have done.

At 48

I swim religiously 5 times a week. I thought I would be done
with it forever when I finished swim team at 21. I began

training again at 27 and have never stopped. I cling to
the idea that I can still swim close to as fast. But, the last

few years, I have had to forcibly gulp in air at the end of sets,
put my head down between my elbows and just swallow it in.

I think this is healthy, as I mutter *Jesus Christ* all the way
to my car. Horribly difficult, this staying 21. I wonder if

my heart can cope, if I can burrow open new coronary arteries
by visualization and flashbacks. If I have a heart attack after

all of this, I will be furious at God, and at the ghostly figure
of my father with a stopwatch. But at least my father will

congratulate me this time for finishing without breathing.
We will laugh and he will hold me and hold me and hold me.

Free loop

The rectangular plastic strip that holds
my excess watchband close to my wrist
begins to break a week ago. Because I swim
for exercise I go through these things twice a year.
The torn area faces me and bothers me
with its indecision. The rip goes about 2/3rds
through the strap, I have no idea how it is still
holding together, but I test it, stretching
it softly like I'm pulling on a black
contact lens or a tiny bat tendon.
It still doesn't give. I suffer
at the incompleteness of the act,
but I don't have time to buy another
one so I let it continue gripping to life,
holding the inside to the outside
with a sinewy tongue of
hope.

It finally snaps the next day
so my niece's pink hair tie holds
it for three days, then I find a wide
rubber band circling wrists of asparagus.
I twist it twice and it provides some awkward support.
Words work this way sometimes. I stretch them
around broken things (or things I define as fragile).
I wrap them around the people
I wish would never come apart,
around my child as I try to keep the spoken skin
we have given her from lacerating.
But these definitions are temporary
and her own words rise out of a sea
of bruises like violet
diamonds.

Leave me be

Last year, my mother fell at 3 AM and my sister,
who lives with her, found her disjointed and moaning
on the floor. At the hospital they discovered she had

fractured C1 and C2, meaning, she was just millimeters
from dying. My sister updated me with the doctors
throughout the surgery. I flew down to HB to see her in rehab,

watched her step unwillingly through curtains of pain
with a walker. She called me by my nephew's name.
I did not mind. Since she has returned home, my sister

explains, the Alzheimer's has been stealing more words
and lucidity from her. If my sister cannot pry her from
the couch where she slowly peels away the thin geography

of her hands, she will sleep, forget to eat.
My mother will repeat, *Leave me be, I am tired.*
My sister implored the doctor to help motivate her

and the doctor replied frankly, *If that is what she wants
to do, you cannot force her.* My sister calls me, tears
float through the phone, choking me. *Maybe he's right.*

But, Scott, we can at least try to get her to swim.
I talk to my mother, say *You love to swim, Mom!*
Yes, I know, Holden, she replies.

I just don't want to.

Another one, or snip

*If you don't want another one,
you should get snipped,* my wife states.
I have given her so many reasons why
I don't want another child, but they
don't ease the crushing in her womb,
in her heart, in her voice, especially
when she squeezes a baby thigh
or holds a plump human to her
ribcage. I love my daughter
to a brutal degree, how can
I open more of that terror
and joy? Besides, I tell myself,
I will be almost in my seventies
when the new child graduates
high school. She doesn't buy it.
She knows it is because I don't
want to go back to the diapers
and endless rocking and singing
of twinkles and cradles and papa sharks.
And our daughter can ski with us now
and I will have to tote a new pupa around
like some elderly stepfather guy
who just stole a bundle and is going
to sell it on the black market.
But she got me with the snip.
To give up the ability to reproduce.
Sure, I still have my parts, but
I would be giving up the functional
part of my youth and instantly turn barren,
spark-less, unusable. *I'm not sure
I want that either,* I argue.
Are you scared of the surgery? she demands.
*No, I am afraid of what it will take from us.
Forever. Give me a little more time.* Time I
do not have. Time we do not
have.

I don't know the name

of the butterfly, but it was fist-sized,
at least, resting on a waxy tropical leaf
in the butterfly exhibit where nets and windows
hold in the 80-degree heat, hold out any
predators. My wife and daughter glanced at it
and kept shifting through, staring at the owl-eyed
wings of the three healthy ones to the left. But
this one I studied, it had become old, much older
than in the natural jungle. Most of us will
eventually be too old like this. The whorls of
cinnamon and coffee had sloughed off most of the wing
on one side and just a lip-shaped top piece held
on by a few threads. The other wing clearly showed
rain splatter from the window behind it. It seemed
to stand calmly, even with most of its life falling off.
I thought, *What did you think it would do?
Panic? Hide? Tremble? Collapse?* It could still
eat, fly—mostly in the direction it wished. It cleaned
itself with its moistening mouthparts and forelegs.
Dignified. Grooming. I no longer felt sorry for it.

In an incubator, emerald and chocolate and paper
chrysalises dangled from wires. Egg, larva, pupa,
and imago. (But what is the stage after imago?)

That night I dreamt pupas sprouted on my sideburns,
eyelashes, pubic regions. My wife didn't notice,
she kept stirring the batter, and shiny pods kept dropping
into the bowl. My daughter blinked her compound eyes,
wiped her proboscis with her forearms gracefully.
Out of the oven my wife pulled a browned pod that
smelled like nutmeg and brie. It opened and screamed
but no sound came, only an open howling
mouth. She handed it to me. It was still
warm.

Let's eat ice cream and fly a kite!
*Velella: free-drifting hydrozoa, which—under the whim of the elements—
may be beached by the thousands*

It becomes a chorus; we all join in because so much
depends on this. Sorry William Carlos, the wheelbarrow
sleeps and we sing! Because she is only 6, because caramel
ice cream sandwiches adorn our hands, because grand drips of now
cascade from the opening sky, because there is wind.
We have a Hello Kitty kite that just might break
in the 30 mile an hour gusts on Nehalem Beach—sea,
a crush of steel glass, sand brailling into our shins.
Molly unrolls the string all the way and the plastic diamond goes up,
nothing to wait for, no more caution, no threat of Hades
coming to snatch Leilani from these Spring pastures
right in front of her mother! Really there is no limit to this, only this:
kite taut, streaking to the moon, Lani's mouth a choir
jumping, arms interpreting straight skyward.

Until, like every short clip on YouTube, it ends, becomes prohibitive
to stay with gristle in the eyes, burn on the ankles. She hands
the pink handle to me, runs to the water, past thousands of silvery
velella bodies cast on the beach. Carcasses, of the many minutes
waiting for water and wind
to bring us here.

My mother calls me

to tell me her mother died.
We visited Grandmother Downes
in the hospital yesterday.
I made a joke about the aqua fluid
flowing into her arm as she slowly
fell away. *What is that stuff,
blue food?* And she laughed.
I didn't want her to see me in despair.
I thought that would make it worse
for her.

My mother told me later
that when she and her sister were
in the room and their mother
suddenly became lucid,
even cheerful, they asked her
Is papa here? She nodded
emphatically and the television
in the room turned on by itself,
blaring noise and color.
Papa had passed many years before.
They asked the nurse why
the television turned on and she didn't
have an answer, and swept out of
the room as quickly as she could.

After my mother called, the phone
rang again. I assumed it was another
one of my relatives telling me
of her death. I said *I know, I'm ok*
before anyone could speak.
Then I listened for a response,
and waited. Nothing but faint
breathing, errant static.
I held the phone for about
a minute, still nothing.
I hung up. I never
knew who it was.

If I had a ticket

to go back to when my father first believed he was worthless,
could I explain to him, in a voice like the groan of an oak,
that worth is not a commodity to be bartered by anyone,
but is intrinsic? Maybe he would listen to himself:
me as a boy talking to another boy, mirrored, half
cellophane, half recorded loop. He made me, he would
have to hear how he was enough, even though adults
made him forget. They too were taught by neglect
amidst long hours working to feed more hungers.
Maybe he would stop having to yell to make sure
everyone could hear his words, repeated
because we weren't answering: mother
hiding behind a Coors, sister attempting
to be worthy for him, in spite of his mirrors,
me trying to scrape the air with salt,
erasers, shame. And the whole
neighborhood could hear—
can still hear.

The way my father ate chicken

revealed the source of his hunger.
He assimilated each leg quickly and thoroughly,
lapping every sinew and hanging thread of its juice.
He glanced at my bones when I set them down
and shook his head. *You missed a lot of meat.*
He was born in 1932, in the middle of the starving.
His father died at age 26 from heart damage
from the Spanish Flu and Strep.
His mother remarried a selfish man who spent
little attention on Lyle, more on a bottle.
His stepfather Gary would refer to him as *the boy*
to his wife while Lyle sat right next to him at the table,
as in *Can you tell the boy to mow the lawn?*
Lyle decided to become more than a third person,
winning student body president at both
Excelsior High and Long Beach State.
He cruised his Austin-Healey with charm,
joined the elite fraternity, visited the UCLA
chapter and stole all their women (he bragged).
He became an English teacher in his old neighborhood
while most of his friends became multi-millionaires.
We still skied with the Haleys in Mammoth,
visited the Malloys on San Juan Island,
but there was always a vacuum in his mouth,
lack in his words. He began to bald, so he spent
nearly an hour each morning spraying
aerosol maple on his scalp and fashioning
his side hair over his crown. I can still taste
the PVP in the air by the three-way mirror.
His glib and profuse words failed to direct his family,
because we had swallowed them too many times.
He turned to shouting. We knew he was still
the president, he didn't need to remind us every day,
with 10,000 words. Of course, we stopped
listening. And in the barking, I heard
the brittle hunger of a boy, two thin bones
on his plate.

Red on the head

like the dick on a dog
is how my father used to describe my hair.
I was probably 10, too young to think
this was funny. He chuckled to himself
and I couldn't look straight at him,
but threw as much cinder and ash
at the side of his smirking face
with my peripheral eye-cannons as I could.
Such disappointment at him for failing
to deliver the minimal respect a child should receive.
Such disappointment at, I surmised,
my own hair.

My mother and father
even bought me *Sun-In* spray.
They would drench my scalp and I was told
to go wander in the sun for 30 minutes—
I pretended to look at the rubber tree,
at the olives dropped in the planter,
at the bougainvillea and its blatant spines
under splashes of vein-magenta.

Then I would wash it out, dry it,
and search my reflection for a difference,
any new gold amongst the rust.
I never cared that my hair
remained the color it was meant to be.
I parted it in the middle, pulled
on my orange Op shirt with wooden buttons
and the matching corduroy shorts.

Took my skateboard out front for hours,
spinning 360s both ways,
hair cutting copper circles in the air,
the air I chose to breathe—
the impenetrable gravity
that I created around myself.
Outside of this, the peroxide sun
burned its skin to tinsel.

Did I tell you the story

of how I quit swimming the first time?
My mother moved the whole family
from our idyllic home in Huntington Beach
to smoggy, fake-greenbelt Mission Viejo,
so I could compete on a premier team.

My father never wanted to go because
it made his commute 40 minutes longer,
but once my mother decided,
there would have to be a divorce
and a shearing of bonds to stop her.

If we don't try, she would say, *we'll never know
if he can make the Olympics.*
My sister, always the hipper kid,
knew that this part of Orange County
would suck the culture out of her marrow

through her sad eyes. And it did.
So, sure, I had some success, but after
2 years I began to die. My father,
after losing many arguments
with my mother, rebelled against his own blood—

all that anger cancerous in its voracity.
At 14 I no longer could stay in the fastest group,
but kept getting demoted to slower
workout schedules, my arms strung bare
with whistling sinews.

One day I decided to stop. I knew
my family had torn themselves up for
my *potential*. I knew the costs.
I sat my parents down and told them.
My father exhaled opalescent spiders

and the smoke which clouds Saddleback
Mountain lifted. We would move back home.
I explained to them that swimming
was mine now, water polo mine,
if I decided to continue competing.

That they could come to the swim meets
but not interfere. I hadn't even hit puberty,
but I grew taller that morning.
At least I owned this defeat,
quietly saying the words,

projecting each syllable as my heart
and lungs and liver and spine
and hands and eyes
woke up and began swimming
in their own bright plasma.

Even though he looked dejected,
I knew my father was proud,
saying to me in his head
*Goddamn it, Scotty, you should
have done this years ago!*

My mother always beat my father at chess

and he would grind every bone in his skull
together until his eyelids sweat. She would

calmly announce *Checkmate* and rise from the table
to concern herself with some new mundane task.

She would forget where she was going in the
supermarket, say, *Oh, that's what I needed,*

and carry on in a half-scattered fashion,
which would lead one to believe her mind

stretched out in many disconnected threads
like a vacant switchboard.

This would lead one to believe that
she could be easily manipulated

or outplayed. Oh—no, no. Ask my father,
he is still sitting at the table replaying ghostly

pawns.

Eggs

My wife grew up glowing and brown
on a Micronesian island where her every effort
returned to her people, her family.
The words *me* and *I* were quiet,
falling into the ruddy current of the Talofofo River
and into the Philippine Sea.

I was anointed white in a coastal town
where, even in my family, I had to consume tacos
quickly to ensure survival, steal the last scoop
of ice cream when everyone else watched
The Gong Show. The word *we* just impeded
traffic, slowed greasy-mouthed satisfaction.

But she has taught me, over years.
Now when I fry eggs for my wife and daughter,
if I break a yolk I know that egg is mine.
I gladly take it. And I know no greater pleasure
than watching them eat the most perfect eggs
I can offer.

Dågan

means butt in Chamorro, the language of Guam,
my wife's home and ancestry. This is one
of several words we have ready when we want to say
things to our daughter without being understood
in Washington. Others are: bebe', vagina, and båba, bad.
You can really stretch out the first baaa in båba
with rotten coconut crab meat in your mouth
to relay your meaning. Baaa as in
Baa baa black sheep, and ba as in *bat*.
I used to struggle with pronunciation,
like saying Mangilao—Mang-ee-low
instead of the proper Man-ghe-lao.
I used to feel the stares of the local men
when I walked into restaurants with
my stunning Chamorro wife on Guam,
*What is that haole doing with **her**?*
coming through the smell of kådun pika.
I have been warned about the Taotaomo'na,
the spirits of the ancestors who will
haunt you and kidnap your children
if you go into the jungle without
asking permission. The ghosts live
in the roots of the banyan trees
which wave at night like blind
esophagus eels.

I know I am a haole, but I have made
a certain contract with the families and roots
of families and old pulsing roots of words.
I can make fina'dene' with plenty of donne'
peppers, the crimson teeth spiking
the soy sauce, and pour it over my rice.
But my skin still burns red, will always burn.
I have learned to cover up.

Sunset through the wires

I have taken pictures of the sanguine
descent of the sun behind Mt. Jupiter and Mt. Constance
from my back deck in blue-collar Renton. Not only
do the Olympics shrink and the novels of blood-cloud
thin to excerpts, but 7 electrical wires bisect the frame.
When I am standing there at 9:30 with my wife,
the dew falling out of the air with faint winds,
bare soles on the cooling wood, we can
imagine it without impediments, without
the 5 trucks on the lawn across the street,
without the tin glow of Benson Center.
We can imagine away many things.
We live in continual imagining,
either that horrors do not exist
because they do not cut us,
or that we are so lucky to actually
own a home we spend 5/7ths of our lives
working to afford. But more conveniently,
we can be content with the canvas before us
by editing it on the way from the optic chiasma
to the visual cortex to the cerebrum to the reward
and satiety centers. We choose, ignore, wash, reflect
any number of actual details. We have different
methods of dealing with discontent. I vow
to fix and clean and dispose and finish.
My wife plans whole new houses in France,
designs campervans with solar-powered escape buttons.
But there are still black scars, children starving,
corporations and memes selling our peace
back to ourselves with interest, the peace
we were born with and have always had,
in and through our light. And if my wife
stands close enough I can feel her and can
frame it all: bile, arsenic, lies, compassion,
forgiveness, grace. And I can still breathe
in her neck and shudder and hold
and breathe again.

After the asking and getting of the things

I left California because everything
about everybody was on sale. Seattle, while pretending
not to care, is the same, except it is not BMWs
and breasts, but Patagonia Nano Puffs
and Subarus. It comes down to satisfaction
and what makes that happen for me.
Do I care that people see me
as successful, hip, congruent
with the Master Culture?
At 49, no. But I do own a Subaru.
But that is not what this poem is about. To a degree
I hinge my feelings of worth and gratification on items.
I work hard, I care for my patients, my family,
I deserve _____. So, of course,
I obsess on that Joel Tudor fin, or those Rome
snowboard bindings, or the ideal hoodie.
I research them, read reviews, check prices,
wait until the coupon code is activated.
It is consuming, the consuming of glorified
idols. I get the thing in the mail, get that
rush of dopamine. Then it needs to happen
again to have the same effect. But
what do I need to order? My family
is healthy, sane, loving. I'm not going
to give everything away and join
a non-materialistic cult, but I could
start one? No. For the first time
in my life I really don't need
anything. And I am thankful.
And I sit and forget to want.
My body doesn't know what
to do, like it is now unnecessary.
I want to molt it off
like an achy sock
and leave it
at the doorway.

Weeds, suffering

The previous owners of this house laid down
fabric and poured in knuckle-sized rock
in a 30 by 20 area of the back yard
hoping the weeds would be eradicated
for decades. Such goals we have against
growth! But red clover tunneled through
the cloth, sprang up like typos, acne. Soon
dandelions, plum tree sprigs, grass, moss,
and many towering shrubs also blanketed the area.
Some say weeding is therapeutic, but they
have never weeded through rock. If I wear gloves
I can't really grip the tendons of root
spiraling sideways. If I don't wear gloves
I get repetitive-use blisters on my thumb.
There are some tasks: draining port-a-potties,
stripping wallpaper, teaching high school English
that can never be made humane. The benefits
are good, people say. And now, I'm a nurse.

So, we planted more invasive species to combat
the unwanted encroachment: golden poppies
and robust northwest strawberries.
Now the poppies scatter garish orange
and the strawberries send out umbilical feelers.
These are infestations we want, we choose them
mostly because people say they are not technically
weeds and they have benefits. But I still have to
grind my knees into the ashen stones and find
things to kill, things that do not meet our criteria.
Editing, or death by lottery. Buckets fill,
blisters form. A bit like a schizophrenic choosing
which images are valid, which are growths
of the mind. We don't really ever know.

Seven pale rocks

It is July and she broke her fever and is sleeping,
auburn skin fluttering over her ribs. Health is precious,
especially when my family and I do not have it.
My child teaches us what is valuable.
But she has her own way of appraising worth.

She had laryngitis yesterday and I found her
in her room quietly organizing her loot: coins,
pearls, plastic and glass beads, broken necklaces,
and a clear box of glinting rock, like feathers of asbestos.
These stones are priceless to her, seven geodes we bought her

for Christmas that she broke open with a heart-sized
chunk of granite. Even in December the slivers of light
rolled out, glowing cities and underground languages
newly spoken. And she gathered them, smuggled
some to her neighbors and school friends, kept the rest.

Yesterday she spilled them out on her floor
with her internal dialogues, *No, you can't take these!*
I hear her proclaim to her other selves in strained words.
Hopefully she will be generous with herself, to herself,
and keep all the voices which break under her feet.

* * * * * *

No, you can't take these! She shouts
at the snow owl who steals words

from the mice so they can't scream
as they are scooped up and swallowed.

She calls on the bobcat queen who
knows all the forest, the worlds under

ground, and the spirit inside the breath.
Can you bring the speaking stones?

She agrees and returns with a glittering box
of whispers. The queen places a tiny

ember in the mouth of each mouse.
Instantly they shriek out in relief

and spring mirrored wings and soar up,
a howling army of flying mice,

shooting light from their eyes!
Frightened, the owl flies back

to winter, past fall and a swirl
of fiery leaves.

Choices

My first reaction when my wife told me my daughter
wanted to quit karate was to force her to go,
like my parents directed me to swim practice.

There were no choices. Why should she have them?
But she was sobbing in the car with her Gi on
unable to go in. I felt that she betrayed me, disobeyed

me, was crying to get out of her duty. But these are my
slivered mirrors, slicing open my fingers as I grip,
my young eyes splitting, my father's eyes.

She achieved her purple belt and beamed.
She wanted to do martial arts to prove that girls
are strong. She had proved that, to herself.

Now she wants to dance. Please, daughter,
dance however you want.
With blinding strength.

Dice, marigolds, molecules

After I built the cedar planters, I found the cheapest soil to fill them because each plot needed 12 bags for a total of 36. I never thought dirt could be so pricey. So, I collected coupons and my wife and I slowly stockpiled the heavy damp slabs and poured them in. All this so we could have vegetables jumping out at us like bounteous confetti. This did not occur. Our pumpkins withered, okra stunted, lettuce dwarfed. While the plants under the cedar tree that were supposed to be languishing sprang to the sky. Again, plans built around assumptions built around luck or some chemistry I didn't know.

So, I poured in expensive fertilizers, organic vegetable foods, transplanted lettuce and squash to different areas according to superstition. Finally, the pumpkins have spread their five-pointed flowers open and bees coated in pollen swim inside and gather. But mostly the result is lackluster: carrot shoots three inches small, garlic shriveled and brown, marigolds the size of quarters. The images in my head were just images. And growth cooperates very little when it is forced. The okra doesn't care how I feel. And the beets wave their pygmy tongues at me under the shade of the one healthy tomato.

Naegleria Fowleri

is the name of the brain-eating amoeba
which worms its way from the tropics of your sinuses

into the electric marsh-plasma of your head. Don't
Neti with tap water. Ok. Wash the C-Pap with bleach. Done.

But what if the pseudopods of each organism were
selective for pain receptors, guilt, shame, loss?

What if old failures tasted like flowing maple syrup?
What if anxiety was as umami as parmesan melting?

What if depression wafted through the dendrites like chocolate,
rich as dried blood? Maybe you don't clean the sterile water

container this morning. Maybe you open the map,
scrawl passwords in red sharpie, arrows pointing

through the sphenoid and into the awaiting
feast.

Keyring

The green carabiner that has hooked my keys
to my beltloop for 10 years finally stops

springing closed, so it keeps clanking to the ground
in the gym, in the hospital hallway.

This metal oval has allowed entry into vehicles
and passages, through nursing school, my wedding

and almost separation, the birth of my child,
through a move to California and back.

I am reluctant to erase it: the dim green tableau
of worn rings and unhinged joints, a fist

of poor dialogue and dark laugh-tracks, now useless.
I finally switch it for a shiny tangerine one,

supple and disconnected to reruns. It frightens me
to know what the orange era will bring.

I'll try to keep the soundtrack silent,
the doors clear as mourning.

Ligaments, death

I popped my knee, she stated too calmly
on the phone. She fell near the top of the run
with our daughter feet away and slowly trudged
her way up 20 yards with her skis to the patrol station.
By the time I flew down and rode the chair up she reclined
in the patrolman's sled, wrapped in an orange blanket. She always
told me that knee wasn't right. Her face shone a smile of someone
who has felt many impacts, and much unjust weightlessness.
The smile said, *Of course this happened to me.*
Lani's eyes sifted inward like sand traps in oil. I explained,
They are going to take her down and care for her in their office.
She asked, *Is she going to have surgery there? Is she going to die?*

Just recently our daughter realized the EpiPen we carried with us
was not going to kill her, but open her airway. We thought we had explained
it many times. She had twirled herself up in our moon-gray
curtains and sang, *I am dead I am a ghost.* We told her, *No, no, do not say that.*
Last summer, entering the threshold of Space Mountain for the first time
she stated, *Well, ok, I'm not afraid to die* as if she had wrestled with the moment
of actual death all night and had resigned her body freely, wistfully.
As if she remembered what it was like to fly through stars.

No, no surgery today. She is not going to die. Let's ski down and meet her.
She didn't cry, but her eyes kept inverting into dark pools, glinting matter
on the other side of matter, as if she could see the edges, or the glowing
gum the ghosts had stuck under the bones of the world.

I guess at the end

of the Huntington Beach Pier
is where my ashes should be showered.
It doesn't matter, except for my daughter,
my wife and the way they remember me.
Maybe Oswald State Park, off the far
cliff by the waterfall. At least they wouldn't
have to fly all the way to California to feel
like they were paying due respect.
The ashes are nothing but ashes.

When my mother and sister and I
loosed my father's remains at the top
of Mammoth Mountain years ago in July,
hikers stepping widely around our
strangely somber frames. I tore
a fingerhole in the plastic bag
and wafted the clouds of sinew
and teeth out over the summit.
The wind swirls back on itself
up there, and his dust flew
into my face as I flapped
the bag up and down awkwardly.
It landed in my mouth
and tasted like Milk-Bone. I didn't
spit it out, it felt disrespectful
to do so. I let it digest. I never
told my family.

The grief didn't stop for years.
I didn't know I was grieving.
I stopped talking as much.
And the rocky edge of that undead
volcano held no magic. But when
I think of him, I feel close to the
elemental feeling of him—
a glow within all the
objects and plans
scattered down below.

Conversation

We never knew my father's relatives, except our grandmother Alice.
Three years after my father died, my sister announced
it was my great aunt Laverne on the phone and that I should talk to her.
Vernie, as she liked to be called, explained that they didn't hear
much from Alice or Lyle after they moved from Iowa to California,
and that she only knew Lyle as a young boy. *I could feel it when he died,*
she stated. I stayed silent. She explained she could usually sense the dead,
that in our family many of the Line surname had this ability,
that her mother Mabel Line Ferry would have casual conversations
with her deceased husband as if he were standing at the end of her bed.
You'll know when I die, she added. I confessed that my father
comes to me in the bathroom, that the walls speak in ether,
that light makes words in the soft flickering. Words
he would say. I don't think I described it exactly that way,
but I didn't need to. *So, you have it too,* she whispered. Yes.

Other things Aunt Vernie told us

That our great great grandfather
stood six foot two and commanded a quiet
respect. That the city of Vermillion, South Dakota
kept voting him into office as mayor
until he retired himself. That he had five sons
who drank, stayed up late,
and earned a reputation for being promiscuous.
Never let your daughter near the Ferry boys
was a phrase learned early in church.
That their mother ran the house
with precision and discipline,
that it wasn't her fault her kids
thought they owned the town.
That all the family had perfect long teeth,
that all the boys could eat through a picnic
in minutes, that you could never follow
them into the outhouse for risk of choking.
That their father lived into his 90s
and he still walked the mile to town
from their farm every day until the end.
That my spooky great grandmother
married his son Phillip and came from Scottish
Pennsylvania, that she still had an accent
thick as Glasgow. That my grandmother
came from a Dutch family from Iowa.
She didn't say how many died from the
Spanish Flu, only that my grandfather
survived enough years to have my father,
even though he was gaunt and frail.
That my father could carry huge bags
of feed on the dairy at a young age,
that he had that Ferry appetite,
that he was bright and quiet and sad.
That she never liked Gary, and knew
she would never see Lyle again
when they drove off. That she was happy
that my sister and I existed, that there
was another Ferry somewhere
consuming all the neighbor's salsa
with flawless teeth.

Pencil drawing from a photograph: the Ploosters ca. 1908

The eyes. I have looked at the original photograph
my sister used for this portrait and it is not
an exact depiction: one face tilts left,
a jawline skews inward, a forearm blurs.
But the eyes float off the flat page,
past the glass a full three inches above the frame.
And they seem to always be inspecting you,
wherever you are in whatever room it is placed.
This picture has graced many walls.
My first wife couldn't stand it.
Maybe the six children saw something
untrustworthy in her movements.

The two boys stand to the left, the youngest
just trying to stand immobile, the older dutifully
looking at the cloaked man giving them orders.
The two middle girls fill the right, the older
with a white bow and cylindrical curls,
the younger with golden hair up and back,
their hands awkwardly still in front
of the lace waists of their high-necked dresses.
The eldest daughter holds the four-year-old
Alice in her lap, her arm both cradling her
and keeping her from crying at the stranger
with the flashing black machine.
At about sixteen her tired but resolute eyes
explain that she cares for her siblings,
cleans for them, cooks for them,
reads to them by an oil lamp.
And my grandmother tries her best not to frown,
her eyes wet and open as smooth eggs
without any shells yet to shield them.

Alice and the plate

My grandmother Alice smoked cigarettes
with trembling hands, kept quiet, peered down.
Her unpleasant husband Gary would recline and watch
Gunsmoke and John Wayne movies all day.
When asked if she wanted dessert,
she always responded, *Just a small piece.*
Her shoulders rolled towards her hidden voice.
Even though she stood 5 foot 8 she took up no space
and blended into the furniture, but her touch
still warmed when she held us,
and her body held a wiry strength.
After Gary died, she lived for many years
independently with her many cuckoo clocks
and china cabinets and the yellow comfort of nicotine.

We heard later that Alice directed calls
as a telephone operator when she was young,
that she stood tall and feline and striking. She was
the only one who could control our grandfather Homer.
He would perseverate on subjects ranging
from the progression of automobiles
to sending photographs through the air
and barrage his listeners with manic rants.
But after he pestered Alice one too many times,
she broke a plate over his head in the kitchen.
That cured him, apparently, and the needle
scratched and lifted off the Victrola.
Our great aunt stated that everyone
was appreciative.

One day before middle school
she sat quietly near me while I listened
to records, this morning it was the Surf Punks.
One song spilled out of the speakers with
boob references and jokes. I glanced
at her and she laughed and laughed
and closed her mouth and laughed
some more. Jesus Christ, Alice,
you were there all along.

When I was 22

my father and I skied together for the last time.
That year I no longer had to remain mostly sober
for swim team, lived in a filthy cocaine and hemp

saturated house in Isla Vista where half of the occupants
imploded their way out of college. I stained my dreads black,
thought I deserved to feel my limbs dissolve with my aspirations.

I had worked so damn hard since age 5 pulling my body
through chlorine for hours, following a straight black line,
playing honors student, mouthing roles.

But you, father, were slowly dying of a type of blood cancer,
and your cheekbones protruded, voice breathed weakly
through words. You took a half a codeine every morning

to mask the malaise. You could still ski,
but complained, *I have to stop every 200 yards.*
Skiing brought the light back into your laboring skin—

it always had. I see you shooting sparks out of your face
even thinking about the coming winter, calling me
in my college apartment, securing dates.

You would start running in October,
wax the Volkls, walk in your Langes,
the illness reduced to a few chemo pills in plastic boxes.

And you kept calling me and I kept downplaying
your survival with flat monosyllabic responses.
I skied with you one run a day and decided your pace bored me,

went off to puff on my pipe between the pines,
sat begrudgingly next to you at lunch,
mostly eating, not speaking much. You even said

I was *lousy company* on the car ride home.
I dribbled my selfishness all over your final active years.
I'm sure you expected something quite different:

your son waiting at every rest spot with the joke
about the man with the apple-sized head
and the beautiful female genie,

recounting together
how you taught him to ski between your
legs while he was still in diapers, and the day

he learned parallel and began to speed away from you.
Not this drugged ungrateful blob.
I admit this is true, yes, and I am so sorry.

So, father, listen, I can finish this. Can you hear me?
The guy in the joke asked the genie
How about a little head? Not funny?

The photograph of you and I holding our skis
in front of the Open Road camper, me four,
all in red, you in brown looking the proudest

I have ever seen you, that picture smiles at my family
every day from our kitchen wall.
That is how your granddaughter knows you.

She skis just as fast as me now.
Hopefully I have a few more years before she races
out to where I can no longer reach her.

Driving from UC Santa Barbara

home to visit my father for the weekend,
my grandmother Alice reverberates through my car
like mourning doves in the fog.

She has been dead 8 years and yet here she is,
not smelling of cigarettes, but of new children's books.
I don't know why I know it is her.

Her son, my father, has been fighting
cancer for 10 years. Recently,
he has begun to lose that fight,

sweating through his sheets at night,
lethargic, blood tests darkening the gray
in his eyes. He lives alone in a condo

next to the beach, a place he has worked
his whole life to grasp. Now his grasp
fails, the ocean no help.

And Alice flushes my neck with
billows of contentment and peace, tears
rolling down to my sleeves.

I tell my father that I felt her come to me when I arrive.
His face pales, eyes look into a distant place.
So, we must be near the end, he concedes.

Michelle and I sit in the meditation room

or whatever they call the room the nurse
leads the family into when someone dies.
Mother weeps over the body, speaking
to the air. Even though they divorced
years ago, they are friends and love
each other dearly.   A calm comes
over Michelle and I, heavy as August,
light as remembering all the reasons why.
I know she feels it too. The release and flight,
the promise of painlessness at the end
of all of the seasons. She turns to me.
He is here, I say.

My sister bought me a psychic reading

and the lovely lady describes the block
in my fifth chakra and how it swallows
up my words before they can escape.
My father barges into the metaphorical
room, because we speak on cell phones.
She stops, stammers, her voice
reveals an edge of bewilderment.
Your father wants to tell you
in no uncertain terms
that you are not going to leave early
like he did. That was his road, not yours.
If you look, both sides of the family
are full of stubborn people
that live a long time.
She laughs, pauses, like someone
just caught her in her bathroom
while she was brushing her teeth,
blared orders at her through a megaphone,
then shut the door again.
That seems legit, I think.
I don't believe she could fake that.

Safety card

We hope you have a comfortable flight
overheard at the end of the safety talk
after they tell you it is unlikely you will need
to use your seat cushion as a floatation device,
and to secure your own oxygen mask before helping others.
I'm sure no one came onto this airplane, this dimension,
this creaking fuselage of a body, expecting comfort.
When have any of us been truly comfortable?
Maybe it lasts 20 minutes.

And this squeezed sedentary reality may be
a fitting metaphor for how we are taught to exist.
You have your assigned seat,
keep your elbows at your sides,
keep your items tucked away.
You are allowed the entertainment we provide,
as long as you pay. If you get up and walk around
in the fake night of pulled shades
you will be scrutinized, and you may impede
the service we provide to others: those prefab hamburgers
cooked five years ago just filling enough so you will shut up
and sleep.

Thank God I brought my own sustenance and my books.
I get up and move about this cabin with the seatbelt
sign on, stretch slowly and move my spirit through
the space and write and design planes without seats.
I dream of levitation, astral projection, omnipresence
on all the continents of our choosing
with huge carne asada burritos
and flowing beer and Crystal tickets
generated from our animated
hearts.

Breathing

Our daughter wrote a simple song
on her new ukulele minutes after she unwrapped it.
She plucked a chord with each word and it rose and fell

and rose and fell. *I love myself just as much as I love you*,
repeated five times. First, I thought, that sounds
vain, she shouldn't say that she loves herself.

Then I said, why not? Hell yes, love yourself.
If my parents had loved me unconditionally
and not for what I had achieved, how I had behaved,

what glory or shame I had brought them, what then?
It is too much tape to rewind. If she can love herself
without having a scorecard, or a language,

or even a paper to burn, what unconstructed music
could pour from her? It could reach beyond
her fingers, her throat, easily careening

over the foothills and across the waters. And inside,
a washing of seas connects, person to person,
and through broken and growing leaves.

Ten words that never knew they were
separate—rising falling
rising falling.

It is April again

so we fill 25 square containers
with compost and seeds and give them
the most direct sun we can, nestled in our kitchen
under the skylights. We spray the fragile shoots
gingerly from above. This morning I drench them, but later
I notice some dry corners, so I pick up the spray bottle
and re-soak the pots.
                      As I set the bottle down this time
I realize it is the pure vinegar we use to clean surfaces,
the acid that kills most bacteria and growing things on contact.
This container is much taller and orange-pink,
how did I confuse the two?
                        I race outside to the shed
and grab a fistful of ground limestone and try to remember
which areas I scorched. I cast the alkaline ash,
like casting bones to repel an impending pestilence.
Should I have scraped off the top layer?
Do I water them now hoping the hydrogen ions
will accept or reject, sizzling to a safe simmer?
The broccoli necks still hold up tiny leaves.
The red runner beans still coil pale under the surface.
I will have to wait. I place the coral bottle on the other side
of the room, protect the new growth from
unconsciousness.
                    Yet, by the end of the week every pot
grows verdant with seedlings, waving like sea anemones.
I have overestimated my power to kill, to control anything.
This is no resurrection. This is no failure. The cotyledons
had already decided to live, their feral roots drinking
with the maw of an ancient God, each with their own name
for the sun.

Early June

When I organized the herb garden,
I cut through the fabric and placed
five Shasta daisy sprouts in the earth—
I never thought they would devour
the space and shoot five feet up.
This morning the first flower opened,
but it was not like those hundreds still fisted
in wax, primate fingers closed in the full sun.
The one that spread awake was tucked
under the rhododendron, shaded
in the margins.

I am totally pregnant!
My wife wakes me with these words.
We have been only trying for two months,
once I finally decided to be a father again.
At least my seeds are still viable at 49.
She radiates filtered elation and fear.
I am prepared, I think, for what is to take over,
how our daughter will react to being overcome
by new growth, replaced with a many-headed
hydra seething from the ground, from our arms.
My wife has wanted a baby for so long. Now.
Now.

We fight about the perfect organization
of the linen closet which I have slowly destroyed
by stuffing mismatched pillowcases into openings.
We argue over wishes being granted too abundantly,
in our beds and in the closets of our minds,
in the foundation where our toes dig in.
The next morning, she asks, *Aren't you scared?*
No, I answer. *I would not call it scared,*
I would call it dread. Dread...but I love you.
We cradle each other. The infant will root
into us and breathe molten light through our skin.
And our daughter will admonish us.
And we will still have to name
all of this.

Acknowledgements

The following poems or versions thereof first appeared in these publications:

"After the buying and the getting of the things" first appeared in *Chaleur*
"Back when I was lying," "Leave me be," and "If I had a ticket" first appeared in *Scryptic*
"Conversation" and "It is April again" in *Noble/Gas Qtrly*
"Eggs" and "Weeds, suffering" first appeared on MoonTidePress.com; *Poet of the Month* feature
"Let's eat ice cream and fly a kite!" in *Toho Journal*
"Ligaments, death" in *Apeiron Review*
"My sister bought me a psychic reading" in *Prometheus Dreaming*
"Sunset through the wires" and "Keyring" first appeared in *Cultural Weekly*
"The only thing that makes sense is to grow" and "Dice, Marigolds, Molecules" in *KYSO Flash*
"The way my father ate chicken" will appear in *MacQueen's Quinterly*
"When I was 22" in *Ponder Review*

About the Author

Scott Ferry helps our Veterans heal as a RN. In past lives he taught English, practiced acupuncture, and managed aquatic centers. He marinated in the vital SoCal poetry scene of the 1990s until he moved to Seattle where he soaked in rain and experienced actual seasons. His work can be found in *Cultural Weekly*, *KYSO Flash*, *Swimming with Elephants*, and *Chaleur*, among many others. He was a finalist in the 2019 Write Bloody Chapbook Contest and a semifinalist in the 2017 Floating Bridge Chapbook Contest. Mostly he tells horrible jokes, tames his garden, and cleans his house. He resides in the great Pacific Northwest and attempts to be handsome enough for his glowing wife and patient enough for his ebullient offspring.

Patrons

Moon Tide Press would like to thank the following people for their support in helping publish the finest poetry from the Southern California region. To sign up as a patron, visit www.moontidepress.com or send an email to publisher@moontidepress.com.

Anonymous
Robin Axworthy
Conner Brenner
Bill Cushing
Susan Davis
Peggy Dobreer
Dennis Gowans
Alexis Rhone Fancher
Half Off Books & Brad T. Cox
Jim & Vicky Hoggatt
Michael Kramer
Ron Koertge & Bianca Richards
Ray & Christi Lacoste
Zachary & Tammy Locklin
Lincoln McElwee
David McIntire
José Enrique Medina
Andrew November
Michael Miller & Rachanee Srisavasdi
Terri Niccum
Ronny & Richard Morago
Jennifer Smith
Andrew Turner
Mariano Zaro

Also Available from Moon Tide Press

Dead Letter Box, Terri Niccum (2019)
Tea and Subtitles: Selected Poems 1999-2019, Michael Miller (2019)
At the Table of the Unknown, Alexandra Umlas (2019)
The Book of Rabbits, Vince Trimboli (2019)
Everything I Write Is a Love Song to the World, David McIntire (2019)
Letters to the Leader, HanaLena Fennel (2019)
Darwin's Garden, Lee Rossi (2019)
Dark Ink: A Poetry Anthology Inspired by Horror (2018)
Drop and Dazzle, Peggy Dobreer (2018)
Junkie Wife, Alexis Rhone Fancher (2018)
The Moon, My Lover, My Mother, & the Dog, Daniel McGinn (2018)
Lullaby of Teeth: An Anthology of Southern California Poetry (2017)
Angels in Seven, Michael Miller (2016)
A Likely Story, Robbi Nester (2014)
Embers on the Stairs, Ruth Bavetta (2014)
The Green of Sunset, John Brantingham (2013)
The Savagery of Bone, Timothy Matthew Perez (2013)
The Silence of Doorways, Sharon Venezio (2013)
Cosmos: An Anthology of Southern California Poetry (2012)
Straws and Shadows, Irena Praitis (2012)
In the Lake of Your Bones, Peggy Dobreer (2012)
I Was Building Up to Something, Susan Davis (2011)
Hopeless Cases, Michael Kramer (2011)
One World, Gail Newman (2011)
What We Ache For, Eric Morago (2010)
Now and Then, Lee Mallory (2009)
Pop Art: An Anthology of Southern California Poetry (2009)
In the Heaven of Never Before, Carine Topal (2008)
A Wild Region, Kate Buckley (2008)
Carving in Bone: An Anthology of Orange County Poetry (2007)
Kindness from a Dark God, Ben Trigg (2007)
A Thin Strand of Lights, Ricki Mandeville (2006)
Sleepyhead Assassins, Mindy Nettifee (2006)
Tide Pools: An Anthology of Orange County Poetry (2006)
Lost American Nights: Lyrics & Poems, Michael Ubaldini (2006)

www.ingramcontent.com/pod-product-compliance
Lightning Source LLC
Chambersburg PA
CBHW031216090426
42736CB00009B/935